D1126331

How to Give a Speech

How to Give a Speech

BY HENRY GILFOND

A Language Skills Concise Guide
FRANKLIN WATTS
New York | London | Toronto | Sydney | 1980

Library of Congress Cataloging in Publication Data

Gilfond, Henry.
How to give a speech.

(A Language skills concise guide)
Includes index.
1. Public speaking—Juvenile literature.
I. Title. II. Series:
Language skills concise guide.
PN4121.G458 808.5′1 80–12738
ISBN 0–531–04130–1

Printed in the United States of America
5 4 3 2 1

Contents

to Pamela

How to Give a Speech

Introduction

It may not have occurred to you, but you have been making speeches of one kind or another for a long, long time. You have probably made many speeches in the classroom, at family affairs, at club meetings, and even to your friends. And almost always there has been a definite purpose to each of your speeches.

In the classroom, for example, you may have been called on to compare the strengths and weaknesses of the North and the South in the United States at the beginning of the Civil War. In that speech, your purpose was to define, to make clear certain differences.

At another time, you may have been asked to name a fictional hero you admire and to give reasons for your choice. In this speech, your purpose was to convince your classmates that your choice was a good one.

You may have been called upon to explain a rule in grammar; to instruct your class in certain procedures, such as the fire drill or the use of a projection machine; or to give a lesson in mathematics. In these cases, the purpose of your speech was to explain, instruct, teach.

Whatever the subject matter, and whoever the audience, the aims of a speech are nearly always the same. Whether you are giving a book report, a social studies report, an election speech, a speech requesting funds from your parents association for football team equipment, or any other kind of speech, you will need to define, explain, make clear, instruct, and convince.

The purpose of this book is to help you develop the ability to make a good speech. It will show you how to find material for your speech, and how to organize that material. It will show you how best to begin your speech, develop it, and end it. It will instruct you in the use of your voice, gestures, rhythm, tempo, and the pause. It will caution you against using worn-out words and phrases and show you how to avoid making some common grammatical errors.

In addition, you will be given some tips on debating—how to prepare for a debate and the techniques of effective debating. Finally, there is a section on parliamentary rules and procedures for meetings, both of which a speaker must understand to function at his or her best before a public audience.

To sum up, this is a book that should help you to make your speeches as clearly, as distinctly, perhaps as dramatically, and certainly as effectively, as possible. Making a good speech is something of an art. It is an art you can learn to use with much self-satisfaction.

Section I. Preparing Your Speech

1. THE EXTEMPORANEOUS SPEECH

There are several kinds of speeches. One is the speech that is prepared in advance. You may have written notes for this speech, or you may have actually written out the whole speech.

Then there is the speech that is devised on the spur of the moment, without any apparent preparation. You may be called on to make such a speech at a family gathering or club meeting, in your classroom, in the school assembly, at a meeting of the school's parents organization, and so on.

You may be asked to make a speech of welcome at a luncheon or a speech of congratulations at a family get-together. You may want to argue for or against a proposal at your club meeting about, let us say, decorations for the annual club Christmas party. In your classroom, your teacher may ask you to explain how you solved a mathematical problem, to speak on different ways to save energy, or to tell why you like or dislike a particular character in a novel the class is reading.

At a parents association meeting, you may be called on to explain more fully the need for upgrading school athletics or to give details on the costs of athletic uniforms and other equipment.

While there is no *apparent* preparation for the extemporaneous speech, no good speech is made without the speaker being prepared, one way or another, to make that speech.

You have probably all heard on radio or television at least one government press conference. Most often, the government official giving the conference opens the session with a short, prepared statement. He or she is then asked scores of questions by the press. The official comes to the conference seemingly prepared to answer all questions. In fact, he or she has prepared very carefully, usually by anticipating all the questions that will be asked and by coming to the conference with all the facts, figures, and arguments that can be gathered in support of his or her views.

The "trick" to responding effectively to such questioning—that is, quickly and convincingly—is to be prepared. You, too, can make a good extemporaneous speech *if* you are properly prepared for it.

You may expect to be called on at a family gathering to make a short speech of welcome, of gratitude, or of congratulations. *Before* you sit down to the table, think of the things you might say. If you are not called on to speak, well and good; if you are, you will not be at a loss for words. You will be prepared.

In the classroom, you must always be prepared to be called on, most often to make a short speech but occasionally to make a long one. Obviously, you prepare yourself for such occasions if you want good marks. The preparation is not difficult. The questions or topics on which you are asked to respond are most often from a homework assignment. The more carefully you do your homework, for the classroom, for the parents association, for the family gathering, or for the clubhouse, the better and more effective your speech will be.

2. THE WRITTEN SPEECH

There are times when you will find it necessary, or even more comfortable, to write out on paper the entire speech you are to make. There are advantages to the written speech.

First, after you have written the speech, you can tell how long it will take you to deliver it. If it is too short, it may not be effective, and you will need to lengthen it. Excessively long speeches, however, may tire an audience and lose that audience for the speaker.

Second, the written speech can help correct misunderstandings about what you said. In the classroom, you may reread your paper to prove that you did *not* omit the Boston Tea Party from your report on American resistance to British taxation; that you did *not* say mechanical failure was responsible for the failure of the space mission; that what you *did* say was that mechanical failure *might have been* responsible.

Third, the written speech permits a more disciplined speech, a planned beginning, middle, and end. The best speeches have a logical development, one point building on another, one idea following another, a proper place for major arguments and minor arguments. We will discuss all these elements later. But obviously, the written speech allows for the more controlled speech.

Fourth, it is easier to make corrections and

changes in your speech when you are writing it down than when you are in the middle of giving it.

Finally, the written speech allows you to review the language and grammar of your speech. We will discuss these elements of your speech more fully later, too. At the moment, let us say you must fit your language (vocabulary) to your audience. Your classmates may appreciate slang; your elders will not. Your peers may excuse certain grammatical errors; your elders will not. Ill-used language or grammatical errors may destroy an entire argument and hurt the effectiveness of your speech.

Let us now examine the different elements of the well-prepared speech. Whether it is a written speech, an extemporaneous speech, or a speech delivered with the aid of notes, the different steps involved in preparing and delivering it are generally the same.

3. OPENING WORDS

You cannot overestimate the importance of the opening words, the first sentences of your speech. These are the words that establish contact with your audience, set up an immediate relationship with it, and set the tone for the rest of your speech.

In preparing your speech give these words special consideration.They must be interesting, of concern to your audience, and demanding of its immediate attention.

At one time or another, you have heard a high government official begin his or her television address with words like:

"I have come here tonight to discuss a grave problem facing the nation."

"I am here tonight to inform you of developments in our oil crisis."

"I have come to speak to you about the pollution that is threatening our nation and the world."

Notice the phrases *grave problem facing the nation*, *oil crisis*, and *threatening our nation.* Each phrase demands our attention. We want to know about the *grave problem.* The *oil crisis* is of deep concern to us. A *threat* to our nation is a *threat* to each of us. Our eyes are glued on the speaker. We don't want to miss a syllable of what he or she has to say.

Your speech is not likely to be so dramatic. Still, the audience can learn something from your opening words.

Put the issue of your speech before your audience at once.

In the social studies class, for example: "Urban blight is rampant in our cities. How do we meet the problem?"

In your English class: "The author of this book accuses the government of high treason."

At your club: "On checking our accounts, I discovered that half our treasury has been wasted on things of no importance to any of us."

To the parents association: "The way we are graded for our schoolwork is old-fashioned. There has to be some change. I have come to propose a new system."

A remark that challenges the concepts of your audience, promises revelations, demands change, or shocks will command immediate attention. You may have pricked the curiosity of your listeners, or even outraged their sense of values, but they will want to hear what you have to say.

Some speakers get immediate attention not with a challenging statement but with a funny story, a humorous remark, or an anecdote. A humorous touch tends to relax both speaker and audience, but you have to be careful with this kind of opening for your speech. If you start with a joke, it may become difficult for your audience to treat the rest of your speech seriously. There is also the question of good taste. A joke will please one audience, offend another. Wit has its place in a speech, but it must be used carefully. We shall talk of this more fully later.

4. MAJOR POINTS

Now let us examine the body of your speech. If your speech is to be a short one, it will generally contain one main idea and perhaps several minor ideas. If it is to be a longer speech, it may have more than one main idea and many minor points. Your emphasis will be, of course, on the main ideas or the main purpose of your speech.

For an example, let us take a speech you might make on the Palestine Liberation Organization (the PLO). What are the major points? Jot them down.

1. Palestine refugee camps
2. The demands of the PLO
3. Supporters of the PLO
4. Terrorism
5. Possible solutions to the PLO problem

Now that you have the main ideas listed, you must decide in what order you will present them in your speech. Do you begin with a description of the refugee camps or with the strident demands of PLO leader Yasir

Arafat? Do you begin with the terrorist bombings or skyjackings or with the hardships of living day to day in the refugee camps?

It would seem that the most dramatic element, the terrorism, would best grab the audience's attention. However, if you begin with a description of life in the refugee camps, you will have your listeners on ground they can relate to. Even if they have no awareness of what a refugee camp is like, they will be able to see how it is alike or different from their own way of living. They will be able to compare and contrast.

As a general rule, whenever possible begin your speech with what is familiar to your audience; then move into what may be less familiar. Give your listeners the facts first, then your opinions, requests, or even demands.

Now would you follow Item 1 with Item 4? There seems to be some logic in moving from the plight of all the refugees to the acts of terrorism committed by some. But you must pause here to ask yourself a few questions. What is the main purpose of your speech? How can you best achieve that purpose? Do you want to defend PLO terrorism? Or do you want to condemn it? Do you want to show the difficulty of finding a solution to the Arab question, or do you have a solution you wish to present?

If, in your speech, you are making a plea for giving aid to the Palestinian refugees, you might omit entirely any mention of PLO terrorism. If you mention the terrorism at all, you will keep it well away from the closing remarks of your speech. However, if you mean to attack the policies of the PLO, you will climax your speech with remarks on the excessive demands of the Palestinians and put considerable emphasis on their terrorism.

In other words, the purpose of your speech will dictate the logical order of the different points in your speech. If you are delivering a talk on, let us say, the life of Ernest Hemingway, you might begin with his birth, go on with his childhood, his schooling, his jobs, the books he has written, and end with his death or his importance as a writer. This is a simple and logical order.

If you are urging your schoolmates to vote for your candidate in the school elections, you might begin with his or her scholastic ability, then go on to the candidate's athletic ability, his or her ability to meet and resolve school problems, and end with remarks on his or her winning personality.

Now let us suppose that while you are organizing this speech you are to make, some new ideas occur to you. Suppose you suddenly realize that you have not considered the effects of the Palestinian issue on other nations, particularly the threat of an oil embargo by countries sympathetic to the PLO. What do you do about this? Can you give the point the time it deserves in the time you have been allowed to speak? If you haven't the time, should you substitute this point for some other point in your speech, and which? Or should you leave out this point entirely and save it for another time and another speech?

These are questions only you can answer, and only after you have considered thoroughly the purpose of your speech and the kind of audience to which you will be speaking.

5. MINOR POINTS

In addition to the major points in your speech, you will undoubtedly have a number of minor points to make. The purpose of your minor points is to develop or support the major points you are making.

For example, to clarify the major point "The demands of the PLO," you might list, as minor points, the historical claims of the Arabs in the Middle East and the historical claims of the Jews to Israel. For the major point "Possible solutions," you might have as minor points friendships between Arabs and Jews, the role of Jordan, and benefits to be derived from a peaceful solution to the problem.

Each of these minor points could easily be developed into a major point. Friendships between Arabs and Jews, for instance, suggest a number of ideas—the history of these two peoples, evidences of friendly relations, friendship between the two groups in your own community. But for the purpose of your speech, you will keep the minor points exactly what they are meant to be, minor. You will use them only to develop or support your main ideas.

In a speech that is a book review, in which one of your major points is the unusual personality of the book's main character, you will support or prove your point by relating relevant episodes in the book.

In an election speech, if a major point is the academic ability of your candidate, your minor points may be the candidate's school average, his or her participation on the debate team, and his or her achievement as director of last year's school stage production. All these minor points, again, will support your major point.

Jot down all these minor thoughts and ideas. How many of them will become part of your speech depends on the purpose of your speech and on the time you will be allowed to speak. Your time limit will also govern the amount of time you can give to each of the minor points you select for your speech. That time must be measured out carefully. While you cannot treat any part of your speech lightly, you must remember to keep a balance in your speech. Minor points are important, but you must always keep your major points in focus. And however interesting a minor point may be, never let it become more important than the main point you are making.

6. CLOSING REMARKS

You got the attention of your audience with your opening statement. You held it with the body of your speech. How you leave that audience will depend on your closing remarks, the last words of your speech.

In your last remarks, you may repeat the major points of your speech, give a summation of your point of view, make a final plea or request, or deliver a warning. The final words should depend on the purpose of your address.

Whether it is a speech for or against a new school constitution, for or against a proposed housing project in your community, a simple book or film review, or a summary of the Palestinian question, your final remarks should include, preferably in the following order, a summation of your main points or arguments, an opinion, and, if appropriate, a recommendation or a plea for action.

Make your last statement as precise and as clear as you can. It should be as forceful as you can make it. Do not bring in any minor points or arguments in your closing remarks.

"I urge you to reject the proposed constitution."

"We need to have more facts before we can support the proposed housing project in the community."

"The film kept me laughing all the way through. It will keep you laughing, too!"

"The Palestinian problem is very complicated, but with hard work, an end to terrorism, and a willingness to compromise, a solution can be worked out."

A good ending to your speech should leave your audience with something to think about. It should, if that has been the purpose of your speech, have charged the audience up and made it eager for action.

The last words in your speech on the PLO might be stirring rather than summarizing:

"There must be an end to terrorism. There must be an end to the suffering of the refugees, too. There is no reason why sane and rational minds cannot effect a just and equitable peace for both Israelis and Arabs alike."

7. SPEECH MANNERS

We have already said that slang may be accepted by your classmates and peers but that it may not go over so well with an audience of older people. Keep this in mind as you prepare and deliver your speech.

Then there is the matter of taste in your vocabulary. There are words and phrases you might use in a doctor's office but that are too technical—or too blunt! —for a public speech.

Be careful also of slander, sarcasm, disrespectful remarks, and self-praise.

Slander, or accusations without supporting facts, will turn an audience against you. Don't accuse anyone of dirty tricks, dishonesty, cowardice, or the like, unless you can prove it on the spot with actual evidence.

Use sarcasm with extreme care. When the brilliant orator Marc Antony, in Shakespeare's *Julius Caesar,* attacks Brutus, Cassius, and Casca by calling them "honourable men," he is being sarcastic. Still, it takes some time for his listeners to understand his sarcasm. Sarcasm, used by a master at speech-making, may prove a weapon to destroy an opponent or an argument. But for someone who is less than a brilliant speaker, sarcasm may very well backfire.

Disrespectful phrases have a tendency to backfire, too. Let us say that, in an election speech, you allude to the unfashionable clothes your opponent wears. While your comment may draw a laugh from those already on your side, the rest of your audience may feel that you are just being nasty, poking fun at somebody who may not be able to afford expensive, new clothes. Instead of winning support for yourself, you have won sympathy and votes for your opponent.

Let others praise you in their speeches. Don't praise yourself.

"I'm the soccer king!"

"I got the new equipment for the science laboratory!"

Singing your own virtues and accomplishments, however valid your song, will not sit well with your audience. More often than not, whatever your intention, your audience will feel that you are simply boasting.

Of course there are times when you have to be a little less than modest, such as when you are campaigning for your own election to school office. At such times it is absolutely necessary to speak of your qualifications and accomplishments. But speak of them as facts, with proof, and, wherever possible, use them to emphasize your beliefs or to show how they relate to your ambitions for your classmates and school.

8. VOCABULARY

Build up your vocabulary. The more words at your command, the easier it will be for you to say what you want to say. And people tend to respect speakers with rich vocabularies. It is the kind of respect that helps to attract and keep the attention of an audience.

You can build your vocabulary by devoting time to using your dictionary. Keep your own "vocabulary book" and jot down new words as you meet them, along with the meaning of those words. Use those new words in your writing and everyday speaking. The more you use them, the more they will become part of your natural vocabulary.

There are many vocabulary drill books in your school library. Borrow them. Such books are intended to develop your vocabulary skills and will surely help in all your schoolwork.

Slang, as we have mentioned, is permissible in your speech at times, and sometimes can be quite effective by adding liveliness to your speech. But slang has a way of fading from spoken language.

How much longer will we say *bread* when we mean money? How much longer will *fuzz* mean policemen? Yesterday's slang is today's *old hat.*

If you are inventive with language, you will find your own, fresher phrases. If not, stick to simpler and more straightforward language.

In another area of your vocabulary, be careful about words that are commonly misused.

Adapt means to make suitable, to fit, to adjust. *Adopt* means to take by choice, to embrace, to accept.

Access means an approach, a way of getting in. *Excess* means too much of something.

A *notable* person is a person to be respected. A *notorious* person is a person known generally for the bad things he or she has done.

To *irritate* is to rub the wrong way. To *aggravate* is to make a bad situation worse.

Watch for these common errors. They can create a subtle but definitely negative effect on your audience. But they can also be easily avoided. The way to avoid such errors is to consult your dictionary for exact meanings, and to remember them.

Proper usage, of course, is a most important element in your vocabulary, but we will discuss that in another section.

9. THE PRECISE WORD

Using the precise word or words will help you to convey the meaning and intention of what you want to say. Words that are not precise may confuse an issue or argument and may damage the message you are trying to put across.

There is a vast difference between *Recognize these facts* and *Consider these facts.* In the first instance, you ask your audience to *accept* a set of facts. In the second statement, you ask your listeners to *think* about them.

There is a difference between *allege* and *assert. Allege* carries the possibility of doubt and the need to prove. In *assert,* neither of these two elements is present. To *assert* is to state positively, without any doubt at all.

"We will *attempt* to change the school dress code." "We will *effect* a change in the school dress code." *Attempt* is a promise of effort. *Effect* is a promise of accomplishment. There is a world of difference between trying and accomplishing.

Words have exact meanings. Be sure you use the exact word for your exact purpose.

A *pretty* girl is not necessarily a *beautiful* girl. A *rugged* individual is not necessarily a *handsome* individual. A *careless* person is not always a *messy* person.

There is a difference between *earn* and *deserve.* You *earn* a salary for work you do, or a scout badge for your scouting accomplishments. You *deserve* credit for your participation in a school project or a rest after long hours of toil.

Is it a citizen's *duty* to pay taxes or is it an *obligation* to pay taxes? *Duty* implies obedience and respect. *Obligation* implies responsibility.

You *respect* the laws of your school, your city, and your country. You *respect* your parents and the flag of your country. You *revere* your church. *Revere* implies awe as well as respect.

To *like* some person is to be pleased by that person. To *love* someone is quite another matter.

You are *restless* when you want to get up and go. You are *nervous* when you are afraid that something of an unhappy or unpleasant nature is to occur.

She cried her eyes red and *She sobbed with grief* mean about the same thing, but the emotions created by these phrases are quite different. Which emotion did you have in mind for your speech?

Precise words and phrases make for precise images and evoke appropriate emotions. Precision helps to convey the speaker's meaning exactly as intended. Finding the precise word and phrase may entail some work, but it is work that will be well rewarded.

10. CUT OUT THE TRITE PHRASE

Just as the exact word and phrase will help your speech, so will the trite phrase, the cliché, detract from your speech. Avoid such phrases as *busy as a bee, out of the blue, more than meets the eye,* and *let me put it this way.*

Such phrases, and the list is much too long, have been heard by all of us again and again, and they mean very little if anything to the audience.

Vivid phrases can spice up a speech and tend to keep an audience alert. But phrases like *it goes without saying, red as a rose, take the opportunity,* and *time marches on* tend to make an audience *tune out!*

What can you substitute for these gray-bearded phrases? That will depend largely on the circumstances of your speech, your topic, and your audience. One approach to creating good comparisons is to refer to a familiar environment:

"As clean as the windows in our classroom."
"As welcome as the last period bell."

You might also consider some common phrases that never seem to die but sound dull to the ear:

Each and every one, when the speaker means, simply, *everyone.*

Last but not least, which generally means nothing more than that the speaker has come to the last item in the speech.

Bitter end, when the end may be very far from bitter.

In this day and age, when the speaker means *now* or *today.*

At one time such phrases probably carried a certain punch and added sparkle to a speech. But today, they've lost that punch and are just flat and trite.

Not everyone has a gift for inventing clever and effective phrases. But all of us can recognize the trite phrase. Take the time to cut out such phrases from your speech.

11. GRAMMATICAL USAGE

Grammatical errors in a speech may have a very negative effect on an audience. This is particularly true when the speaker is well schooled and is expected to speak the language correctly. Obvious errors in grammar tend to cast doubt on the intelligence of the speaker and on the importance of what is being said.

Let us look at the more common of these errors.

I is used as the subject of a sentence. *He and I worked out the problem.*

Her letter was sent to me. Between you and me. Me is used as an object in a sentence.

The same rule must be applied in the use of *he and him, she and her,* and *they and us.*

Another common error crops up in the use of *doesn't* and *don't. He, she, or it doesn't. I, we, or they don't.* If we didn't use the apostrophe, it would be *He, she, or it does not. I, we, or they do not.*

You *lie* down. You *lay* the cloth on the table. *Lie* means to assume a position. *Lay* means to give position. The difficulty with these two words is that *lie* is an irregular verb, and no word is more misused in the English language.

Lay is a regular verb. Now I *lay* the cloth on the

table. Yesterday I *laid* the cloth on the table. Tomorrow I *will lay* the cloth on the table.

It is quite different with *lie.* Now I *lie* down. Yesterday I *lay* down. Tomorrow I *will lie* down.

It is not really that complicated. Just remember *lie* means to assume a position, *lay* means to position.

Other common grammatical errors: You don't dive *in* a pool, except when you are already in the pool. Generally, you dive *into* a pool. You can't divide an apple *between* three people; you divide it *between* two and *among* three.

The balloon is not *liable* to break; it is *likely* to break. It is *this kind* or *these kinds.* It is always, *He plays well,* never *He plays good.*

There are many other common grammatical errors or mistakes in usage. Check for possible blunders in your speech by referring to a grammar handbook. The effectiveness of your speech will benefit from the care you have taken with grammatical usage.

12. VISUAL AIDS

While preparing your speech, you might consider the use of visual aids: pictures, graphs, charts, slides, a blackboard, maps, and more. You have heard people say that one picture is worth a thousand words. That's not always true, but pictures can often help you make the points of your speech faster, clearer, and often more dramatically. Let's consider some of these visual aids, and how best to use them.

First, the picture, graph, or chart must be large enough to be seen clearly by your audience. Before you deliver your speech, test the size of your visual aid by standing in back of the room as well as on the extreme sides.

If your speech is about famine, you might want to use maps and charts. But if you are making a plea for aid to children dying of starvation somewhere in the world, you may instead try to obtain news photographs and have them enlarged. In pleading your cause, you will want to be certain that even people in the last row of your audience can see the ravaged faces and bodies of the victims.

If you are speaking to the parents association, asking for additional funds to support school athletics, your graph might indicate the rising costs of equipment. This might be a bar graph or a line graph. In either case, you will want the bars or lines, as well as the numbers, to be plainly visible to your audience.

If you use a blackboard during your speech, be sure that whatever you write on it—names, dates, graphs, etc.—is large enough and that your chalking is heavy enough to be seen far away. Test the chalk you are going to use before you start to speak. When possible, do the chalking for your speech in advance, before you get up to talk. If the blackboard is movable, turn it around, its face away from the audience; you can turn it back when you are ready to show your listeners what you have on the board.

The blackboard can be a very useful piece of equipment. As you go along you can erase what you have written and replace it with material more pertinent to the latter parts of your speech. Or you can simply add to what you have written. This is a very good technique to use in a speech that is meant to teach a process such as developing film or finishing wood. As you describe the steps involved, you can put them on the board for emphasis and to keep the different steps in proper order.

It is sometimes a good idea, in using the blackboard, to employ different shades of chalk. This is especially helpful when you are using the blackboard for graphs. The different hues sharpen differences and carry your point across to your audience more clearly, more vividly, and often more dramatically than black and white does.

If you use pictographs (picture graphs) to show, let us say, the growth in the use of over-the-counter drugs over the years, be sure that the pictures are as simple as possible. You want the pictograph's meaning to be grasped quickly by your audience. Again, use different colors in your pictograph to dramatize the point you are making.

Slides and filmstrips offer an abundance of visual possibilities, with one important drawback. The film projector and the slide projector require a darkened room, and a darkened room hides the speaker from the audience. The film and slide may aid the speech, but they subtract from the speech-maker. If you have an overhead projector available, you are fortunate. The overhead projector may be used in a lighted room; thus the speaker can remain visible to the audience. This is most important. Whatever aids you use, you, as the speaker, must remain the most important object in the room. For that reason, even when you use film and slide projectors, try to arrange to have a small light on you, so that your audience will know that you are still with them.

There are other precautions you must take when using visual aids.

For example, if you are right-handed, it is best to stand to the left of your visual aid while you are showing it to your audience. If you are left-handed, you should stand to the right of your visual aid.

Never stand in front of your visual aid. You don't

want to block your audience's view of it. Also make sure you won't have to jump from side to side to be sure everyone in the room can see what you are showing them. Unnecessary movement can be very distracting.

A pointer can help you with your visual aids. It will keep you at a good distance from your aid, allowing you a fuller view of it. It will also enable you to point out to your audience a particular name, figure, face, or whatever, without blocking the rest of the aid.

Never use your pointer to gesture; use it only to point out something specific on your visual aid.

And always remember that the visual aid is secondary to your speech; it's an aid and no more. It certainly is not your audience. The most common mistake speakers employing visual aids make is to forget the audience for the chart or graph or picture on the screen or blackboard. Much more often than not, in such cases, the speaker will face the visual aid and, forgetting the audience, will make the speech to the visual aid.

Use your pointer to indicate the aid, but don't look at the aid any longer than you need to. Turn back to your audience as quickly as you can. Keep contact with your listeners. Visual aids can be very helpful, but never let them separate you from your audience.

13. OTHER AIDS

Visual aids are by far the most common types of aids used in giving speeches. However there are times when you may want or need to use other aids in your presentation. Perhaps you wish to bring chemicals to demonstrate some physical phenomenon or a tennis racquet to demonstrate the backhand grip. You may even be called upon to show how to bake a chocolate cake, in which case you would need pots and pans and mixing bowls along with the ingredients.

These aids can be very useful to the speaker and are sometimes a necessity. But use them sparingly. As with the visual aids, do not allow them to become more important than what you have to say. Remember, an aid is an aid to your speech, not the speech itself.

14. SELECTING A TOPIC FOR YOUR SPEECH

Most often you are assigned a subject for your speech. But if you are given a free choice of topic, here are some suggestions on how to select a good one.

1. Choose only a topic that interests you, perhaps some aspect of aeronautics, a hobby, some current event, or any subject in which you have discovered interesting reading material. You probably already have some facts and figures on hand concerning a topic you care about, and, more importantly, since you are already interested in the subject matter, the chances are that you can more easily gain and hold your audience's interest.

2. Limit the scope of the topic you choose, using your time allotment as a guide. If you have no more than fifteen minutes to talk, don't select as your topic *Inflation* or *The Juvenile Justice System.* You couldn't cover either of these subjects unless you had hours and hours in which to deliver your address. Instead, if you are particularly interested in these areas, you might limit your talk to an explanation of wage and price controls or to the pros and cons of trying youthful offenders in adult courts.

3. Consider your audience. Would it prefer a talk on nuclear energy or one on disco dancing? Would it be more interested in your tour of Europe or in your backpacking trip through the Canadian wilderness? Would it be more attentive to a speech on tracking a tropical storm or one on athletic scholarships for girls?

Know your audience. Know what will interest that audience. And choose the topic for your speech accordingly.

Following shortly are some suggestions for speeches you might want to make. They are divided into several broad subject areas.

You will notice that among the suggestions are a few that are controversial in nature; that is, there is considerable difference of opinion on, for example, whether marijuana ought to be legalized, the value of vitamins, and so on. Such subjects not only make for interesting speeches, but they can also be used in debates. We will discuss debates in a later chapter.

One final word before presenting the lists. Keep in mind that these are only suggestions. Many are usable as they are given, but others span broad areas, broader than you could cover reasonably well in a short speech. The function of these lists is to help you think of related topics, topics perhaps more manageable, more familiar, or more interesting to you. The lists are relatively short, but the number of speech possibilities is endless. It is up to you to narrow down or focus on a topic that will not only be right for you but will be acceptable to your audience as well.

Science

a. Recent developments in cancer research
b. Black holes in the universe

c. The CAT scanner
d. The value of vitamins
e. Special diets for teenage diabetics
f. What can be done with atomic wastes?
g. Cloning experiments
h. Electronic video games—what next?

Social Studies
a. Islam in politics
b. Hunting down Nazis in hiding
c. Women as heads of government
d. Oil politics
e. Does Vietnam still affect us today?
f. Should our military budget be cut?
g. The building of the first transcontinental railway
h. Fighting the rise of terrorism in the world
i. Whatever happened to the population explosion?

English
a. Modern black writers
b. The most liberated female in fiction
c. Some poetry I will never forget
d. Should we be required to memorize poetry?
e. How does television affect reading habits?
f. Should student newspapers be censored by adults?
g. What is tragedy? comedy?
h. How to write a successful research paper

General
a. What's new in aviation?
b. How smoking is harmful to your health
c. The greatest football game ever
d. The most expensive stamp in the world
e. Should schools teach sex education?

f. Have we been visited by UFOs?
g. The strangest records ever broken
h. Windmills and energy
i. Should marijuana be legalized?

15. RESEARCHING FOR YOUR SPEECH

Once you have decided on the topic for your speech, you will have to collect some facts and figures. The library, of course, is where you go to get them.

Libraries have a number of different encyclopedias that will provide you with much of the basic information you will need. There are also many books in the library on individual subjects. Finally, the library houses stacks of magazines, periodicals, and newspapers that will provide you with the latest information on the topic of your choice. And if you have any difficulty locating the material you want, a librarian is there to help you.

Once you have all appropriate material collected, you can jot down all the facts and figures that directly relate to the speech you have in mind. You may also wish to write down quotes by important people or phrases that strike you as particularly effective. Be sure to write these down word for word. For the rest, it is better to write down in your own words what you have learned from your references. These words will have more meaning for you when you are at home, away from the original text. It is also a good idea to jot down the books, magazines, and page numbers from which you got your information. You may need these items as evidence in an argument of your speech. And always credit a direct quote in your speech.

16. ORGANIZING YOUR SPEECH

Once you have the notes for your speech ready, you can begin to organize the body of that speech.

Let us suppose you have decided to deliver a talk on the development of air travel. You might list your major points as follows:

I. Early experiments
II. The first successful flights
III. From the Wright brothers to the supersonic jet
IV. Experiments for future air travel

But you realize early on that this is a very broad topic and would require many hours of speaking to cover effectively. So you decide to limit your topic to *Early Experiments in Aviation.* Then your major points might be:

I. The first French flyers
II. The German zeppelin
III. Failures
IV. The Wright brothers

You will note that each outline has a logical order, from yesterday to today, from today to tomorrow.

Now that you have the major points, you must list the possible minor points in the order they belong. Let us take the section on the Wright brothers:

IV. The Wright brothers
    A. The bicycle shop
    B. The man-carrying kite
    C. Kitty Hawk

The major points have been designated with Roman numerals, the minor points with capital letters. You can develop this outline even further, listing items that explain or further develop a minor point:

IV. The Wright brothers
    C. Kitty Hawk
        1. The glider
        2. Early failures
        3. Success

With this sort of division and subdivision, you will have blocked out your entire speech. Now assemble your notes according to each division and subdivision in your outline.

With all these preparations done, you are ready to write the first draft of your speech.

You might begin by devising a good opening sentence or two.

"There was a report in the papers, a few days ago, of a new ultrasonic plane that can cross the Atlantic Ocean in less than three hours. We have moved a long way from the first flight at Kitty Hawk."

"The first men to try to fly in the skies were men of vision. They were also daring and brave, risking their lives in an effort to imitate the birds."

A dramatic opening sentence isn't always possible or even necessary, but it certainly helps get the attention of your audience.

Once you are satisfied with your opening remarks, go directly to your outline. The outline is the guide, the blueprint, for your speech. Never lose sight of this outline as you organize the notes you collected in the library and as you write your speech.

When you have finished writing the body of your speech, you must then compose your closing remarks.

You will recall that we said the closing remarks should sum up your talk and, if it is called for, your opinion or a special plea. In your talk on *Early Experiments in Aviation,* there is obviously no need for a plea. However, after you have briefly summarized the major points of your speech, you might want to mention some of the men and women who carried forward the heroic work of the Wright brothers:

"Since Kitty Hawk, men and women like Captain John Alcock, Lieutenants John Macready and Oakley Kelly, Lieutenant Commander Richard Byrd, Amy Johnson, and of course, Charles Lindbergh and Amelia Earhart have made aviation history. One could profitably read their stories also."

Or you might want to carry your audience into the present day:

"The supersonic transport jet crosses the Atlantic, from New York to Paris or London, in about three hours. It is not difficult to imagine that, with the steady development in aeronautics, even that record will be beaten, and in the not-too-distant future."

Notice that you have ended your speech dramatically and left your audience with something to think about.

The first draft of your speech is just that. It is not yet a finished speech. Before you are ready to deliver your talk to an audience, you must do some editing.

17. EDITING YOUR SPEECH

You must now read the speech aloud to be sure it isn't too long for the time you have been allotted or too short. If it is too short, find something in your notes you can add to the speech. If it is too long, look for places where you might cut. Cut out all unnecessary repetition. Cut some of the examples you may have given for a particular aspect of the speech. For example, talking about two attempts of the Wright brothers that failed, instead of three or four, may be all you need for your speech.

Cutting, in any case, generally helps a speech. It tightens the speech and tends to quicken its tempo.

Next, make a close study of your vocabulary. Have you always used the precise word? Have you included any trite expressions? And remember to avoid abusive language, slander, and sarcasm in all your speeches.

Then check for grammatical usage. Be sure you haven't made any of the common errors we have already discussed.

Now read your speech again. Are you really satisfied with it? Remember, it is much easier to make corrections in your speech before you deliver it than while you're giving it.

Section II. Delivering Your Speech

In this section, we will discuss the preparations necessary for the delivering of your speech, then the techniques involved in speaking to an audience.

Let us begin with a discussion of the appearance of the speaker.

1. APPEARANCE

First impressions may not be lasting, but they can be very important. It is the *appearance* of the speaker that the audience responds to first. A good appearance will immediately attract an audience, get its attention, and, often, encourage a sympathetic attitude even before the speaker speaks the first word of the speech.

A well-groomed, neat, and appropriately dressed speaker will command a certain respect from the audience. Different audiences and different circumstances, though, call for different dress. You won't put on formal clothes—a suit or a dress—just to deliver a report to your classmates. But you might do just that if you are to deliver an address to the parents association. You might wear jeans and a sweater to address a football rally but not to give a formal speech at a dinner or banquet.

Of course whatever your speech and audience, your hair, no matter how long, must be clean and combed. Your clothes don't have to be new, but they must be clean and pressed. Your shoes always look better when they are polished. You may be as casual as you like, if the occasion allows it, but no audience will excuse a lack of cleanliness or a messy appearance.

2. POSTURE

Your posture, the way you walk and the way you stand, will also be noticed by your audience. It will affect the way the audience responds to both you and your speech.

From the moment you are called to the front of the room to make your speech, the eyes of the audience will be upon you. Your audience will observe how you get up from your seat, how you walk to the platform, how you mount the stairs, how you approach the middle of the stage. The way you rise, walk, and take your position on stage are all part of your introduction to your audience. It gives your audience a sense of what to expect from you. Your posture, at such moments, will go a long way toward establishing the tone and mood of the audience's reception or reaction to your speech.

Don't jump out of your seat. Don't crawl out of your seat. Just stand up, as you normally would. Make it seem as if being called to speak were nothing new for you. Take whatever papers you need for your talk, and proceed at once to the speaker's platform.

The walk to the speaker's platform nearly always seems longer than it actually is, but if you keep yourself straight and tall, with your shoulders back but relaxed and your head up, the walk will seem to be just a bit shorter.

Actually, the moment you are called upon to speak, your adrenalin will start flowing. It happens with even the most professional of speakers. Your heart will begin to pump a bit faster and, if you are like most people, you will feel nervous.

What can you do about this nervousness? Not too much. But knowing and rehearsing your routine beforehand will help. Try standing up from your seat. Try walking to the front of the room. Are you holding your head up and standing and walking erect?

On stage, maintain your posture. Avoid leaning on the table or the lectern. Keep your hands off anything you don't need for your speech. The easier your manner, and that means your posture, the more confidence your audience will have in what you say.

Onstage posture may be worked on, too, in your own room before a mirror. And the more you rehearse, the better you can control the manner and effectiveness of your speeches.

To sum up, stand straight, head high and shoulders back but relaxed, walk naturally, use no unnecessary props, and carry yourself with the dignity of a speaker who is prepared and pleased to speak.

3. VOICE

Your voice is the instrument with which you speak. Some people are blessed with magnificent voices. You have probably often been impressed by the richness and depth of the voices of radio or television announcers. It doesn't seem to matter what they say; they make music that pleases.

What kind of sound does your voice make? Have you ever really heard it? Our ears do not give us the true tone of our own voices. The only way to get the true tone is by recording or taping your voice and then replaying the record or tape.

You will probably be surprised when you hear your recorded voice for the first time. Your pitch may be higher or lower than you thought, the tone deeper or thinner than you imagined. And you may be equally surprised by your diction and the projection of your voice.

No matter, this studying of your voice on tape is a good first step in the improvement of your speeches.

If your voice is too high pitched, you will discover that by speaking more slowly you can bring that pitch down. Similarly, if your pitch is too low and you want to bring it up, speak more quickly. Try it and see.

If your voice is harsh or strident, it is probably because you are tense. You need to relax.

How do you do that?

First, relax your posture. When your body is relaxed (not flopping about, but relaxed), then your voice will emerge more smoothly and naturally.

Second, try to improve the quality of your breathing. When you inhale and exhale properly, you speak better. Good breathing exercises, taught on many yoga records, will help.

Third, remember that you speak better when you are not emotionally upset—when you are not angry, afraid, excited, depressed, too exuberant, or badly disappointed. Test yourself using a tape recorder. You will soon hear the importance of keeping calm and collected when you speak.

To sum up, use the tape recorder to evaluate your speech, then work (1) to eradicate whatever faults you find and to improve those qualities of your voice that please you; (2) to develop good, natural breathing; (3) to develop and maintain good posture; and (4) to be as calm as possible whenever you are making a speech.

4. DICTION

Speak clearly and distinctly. Mumbling, slurring, or swallowing your words are simply lazy speech habits and do not make for effective speaking. These habits can distort or even destroy the meaning in your speeches. You have something to say; be sure that your audience hears it as you mean it to be heard.

Say carefully each word you speak. When you say *one, two, three,* be certain it is heard as *one, two, three* and not *one to three.* When you want to say *singled out,* be sure it doesn't come out as *single doubt,* perhaps confusing your audience completely.

A countless number of people out of laziness do not pronounce their *t's* and *d's.* How often do you hear someone say *tweny* or *twendy,* when the word intended is *twenty?* How often have you heard *decied,* when the word intended was *decided?*

Another common error in diction is the *ng* ending in words. It's *sing a song,* not *singa song.*

Be sure you don't forsake the last letters of your words. It's *evening,* not *evenin.* It's *Don't do it,* not *Don do it.* It's *hot day,* not *ho day.*

You can catch these kinds of errors by listening to a tape of your speaking. They are the kinds of errors that are easily discovered and effectively corrected by drills and practice.

Discover your errors, if you have any; work on correcting them, using your tape recorder to check your progress; and see how quickly you can overcome faults due to laziness.

There are more serious faults in diction, faults that may require some special attention.

Do you lisp? Do you speak through your nose? Is your voice too guttural? Do you stammer?

Here the fault may be due to something physical, or even psychological. If you suffer any of these faults in diction, you would do well to consult a speech-teacher in your school. In most cases the speech-teacher will be able to diagnose the cause or causes of your specific problem and will prescribe a set of exercises to help you overcome it. If you do those exercises diligently and check with your speech-teacher or a speech therapist regularly, your speech may improve a great deal in a short time.

For most of you, however, it is good to know that most faults in diction are due primarily to lazy speech habits; and these, with a little attention and some corrective exercises, can be quickly overcome.

5. BEFORE YOU MEET YOUR AUDIENCE

There are a number of things you can do before you actually step out to meet your audience, things that will help you feel more comfortable and thus enable you to deliver the best possible speech you can.

First, you should rehearse delivering your speech. You might want to memorize it. Committing the speech to memory will permit you to look at your audience all the time you are speaking. And eye-to-eye contact with your audience makes for a more friendly, intimate relationship between a speaker and his or her audience.

However, there are a number of disadvantages to memorizing a speech.

First, it takes time, time you may not be able to afford or want to spend.

Second, a memorized speech tends to make for a stiff, mechanical performance.

Third, should you lose a paragraph, a sentence, or even a word of the memorized text, you may very well be thrown off balance. You will stumble and fumble for the missing thought and the good effect of your speech may be entirely lost. A momentary interruption in your speech, caused by some noise in the audience or in the street, or even by audience laughter or applause may well have the same devastating effect on your memory and your talk.

Instead of memorizing the entire speech, it is probably better to simply memorize the outline for it. If you do this, you will only occasionally have to look down at your notes, perhaps to recall a specific figure or piece of data. Your speech, too, is likely to sound more spontaneous.

In any event, it is a good idea to memorize both the opening and closing remarks of your speech.

Rehearse your speech in front of a mirror. You can tell then whether the gestures you are inclined to make are suitable and not overdone. You may point a finger to make a point, but if you point that finger too often, it loses dramatic value. Similarly, you may make a fist to emphasize a point in your speech. But clench your fist too often and that clenched fist becomes meaningless. Generally, you should limit the gestures in your speech; the fewer the gestures the more meaningful and dramatic they are.

Examine the room in which you are to make your speech. Become familiar with it. Try to determine just how loud you must speak to be heard by everyone in the room. If there are any impediments in the room, such as a concrete column that may obstruct the view of some of your listeners, try to figure out a way to overcome the obstacle. You may have to change your position, moving occasionally from side to side so that everyone in the room will have a chance to see you.

Listen to the noises outside the windows of the room. Some street noises can be very distracting and disturbing to both audience and speaker. If you are aware of the nature and extent of those street noises before making your speech, you will be better prepared to deal with them. You will be ready to pause in your speech to let that plane overhead pass. Certainly you should not attempt to talk over any loud noise.

Walk around the room several times till you feel you know it and are at home in it. This will help to relax you for when you meet your audience at last, and a relaxed speaker is a better speaker.

6. MEET YOUR AUDIENCE

You are called on to speak. However well you have rehearsed, your heart will suddenly begin to beat fast. You rise from your seat and advance to the front of the room or the speaker's platform. Of course if you are being called on to receive an award, you might wave a hand to a friend, someone in your family, or your coach. Generally, however, you make straight for the speaker's dais.

The butterflies are probably dancing in your stomach. Your hands have begun to sweat. You discover you are not breathing too easily. It is all the result of a natural tension, nervousness.

Take a deep breath. Hold it. Then let it go slowly. It is amazing how quickly your breathing becomes normal, the sweat subsides, and the butterflies leave you. A big yawn would help, but you can't yawn while you move to the speaker's stand.

At the stand, take another deep breath. Hold it. Release it slowly. This is a speaker's trick that never misses.

"Mr. Chairman." (or "Ms. Chairwoman.")

Those are your first words. They are expected of you. They constitute a common courtesy. If there are special guests in the audience, you give them the same courtesy.

"Mr. Chairman, Councilman Newton, Reverend Turner, and distinguished guests . . ."

Then your audience, ". . . friends, parents, ladies and gentlemen."

These first words are a salutation to your audience and exactly what they are depends entirely on the nature of your audience. When you make a report in the classroom, no salutation is necessary. But even at a clubhouse meeting, this kind of formal salutation never hurts. On the contrary, it adds to the dignity of the speaker and the importance of the speech.

Following the salutation and perhaps another deep breath, you move into your speech.

7. PROJECTION

To be certain that every word of your speech is heard, you will need to project your voice into the audience. This you can easily learn to do.

First, stand erect and relaxed. The erect body delivers the voice with more power and control. The relaxed body is free of the tensions that tighten the throat and prevent it from sending out the voice naturally and clearly.

Second, keep your head up, not stiff, so your throat is open and clear for your voice.

Third, keep your feet flat on the floor. If you waver or jitter around, the audience will be distracted or wondering when you're going to fall over instead of listening to what you have to say.

Fourth, keep your arms and hands loose and natural. Gesture only when you need to. A speaker with nervous arms and hands will have the audience concentrating on those arms and hands, not on the speech.

Fifth, and this was mentioned earlier but bears repeating, don't hold anything in your hands you don't need for your talk. You may need your written speech or notes or even a pointer. But don't play with a pen or pencil. Don't play with the buttons on your suit or shirt or dress. Don't run your fingers through your hair.

And while we are concerned with don'ts, if you are chewing gum, get rid of it before you reach the speaker's stand. Nothing disturbs an audience, any audience, more than a person chewing gum while talking.

8. LOOK AT YOUR AUDIENCE

Don't look at the floor or the ceiling or the windows of the room as you deliver your speech. Look at your audience.

If you are reading your speech or need to consult the notes you've prepared for your speech, make a point of looking out into your audience as much as possible. It is important to maintain eye-to-eye contact with your listeners. You want them to feel that you are talking to them, not to the papers on your lectern.

Find a friendly face in the audience when you start to speak. Speak to that one person directly. The feeling that you are talking to just one person will make you more comfortable on the dais, especially if you are not used to addressing a large group.

Find that friendly face somewhere in the middle of your audience, and your listeners won't be aware of your concentration. It will look as if you are speaking to all of them.

After a while, as you grow more comfortable with yourself, you will find yourself looking at another, then another friendly face in your audience. This will all come about naturally. Most audiences *are* friendly.

9. TONE, TEMPO, PITCH

Every now and then, change the tone, the tempo, even the pitch of your speech. A speech without change of voice becomes monotonous and puts an audience to sleep.

How do you change the tempo? You speak a little faster or a little slower. The speed with which you talk, as we have already noted, determines its pitch. Speak faster and your pitch goes up. Speak slower and your pitch goes down. The tone of your speech should fit the words you speak. If you are attacking in your speech, your voice will be more harsh; if you are defending, it should be softer.

You change your tone, tempo, and pitch to emphasize a point in your remarks or to ask a dramatic question:

"They have systematically destroyed our natural resources!"

Or, "Shall we allow them to systematically destroy our natural resources?"

You change your tone, tempo, and pitch when you want an abrupt change in mood:

"I was given this prize for exceptional ability in mathematics. *I do not deserve it.*"

These changes will keep your audience alert, but don't overdo them. Time them properly or else the changing itself will become monotonous.

10. THE PAUSE

The pause is an excellent device for a speaker. It can often say more with its silence than could be said with words. It can also serve to give the speaker a breather and allow time for the speaker to collect his or her thoughts or to measure the mood of the audience. Of course a pause must be meaningful.

For example, you pause before a rhetorical question to give your audience time to realize the importance of the question:

"Are we going to take all this lying down?"

The "No!" you want may not be spoken, but the silence of the audience during that pause can be very dramatic.

You pause after making a telling point:

"Arson has killed more than a hundred men, women, and children in this country in only the first two months of this year!"

The pause allows the idea to sink in, and the horror and waste of arson becomes more apparent.

You will pause, too, for less dramatic reasons. There is an unexplained noise backstage. Pause until the noise subsides. A fire engine with its siren screaming moves down the street. Pause until the noise has passed. The audience is amused by something you said and laughs. Pause until the laughter has almost died down. The audience applauds something you have said. Pause until the applause comes to a stop.

The less dramatic pauses are the ones you do more naturally. You pause each time you have made a summary of a major point and before introducing your next major point. This pause is like a signal for a new paragraph. It allows your audience to think about, if only for a moment, the major point you have just made.

The more dramatic pause, again, is an excellent device for your speech. But use it sparingly and wisely for its best effect. If it is overused, it will lose its impact.

11. GESTURES

Use gestures to stress a point or add a dramatic touch. You may point a finger to show the way or to accuse, or throw up your hands in a sign of despair. You may smile to show approval or frown to show disapproval. The gesture will reinforce whatever you are saying.

However, as we have already indicated, too many gestures will spoil a speech, water down its effect.

Another caution: Gestures should be natural, never mechanical. Be particularly aware of this when you rehearse your speech at home, in front of your mirror. Unnatural, mechanical gestures will lose you the audience's respect.

Like the pause, use your gestures sparingly. Make them count.

12. WIT

Wit may serve a speaker well, too. But, like the pause and the gesture, use it sparingly and cautiously. Remember that what may be funny to you may not be funny to your audience.

What makes an audience laugh?

Sheer nonsense: A funny hat. Putting an unopened can of tomatoes into a stew. Walking around a ladder instead of under it, only to fall into a manhole.

Shaggy dog stories, stories with nonsense endings: A man is told he is wearing carrots on his head and answers, "Oh! I thought it was spinach."

Puns. Playing with words: "There's too much Greece in this Turkey."

Humorous spots in your speech may help warm up an audience, relieve tension, or provide a welcome pause in the seriousness of your talk. But they must be used with extreme care.

Here are some precautions.

(1) Don't announce a funny story in advance. Your audience may not think it as funny as you promised it would be.

(2) Don't give away the point of your story before you begin to tell it.

(3) Don't drag a story into your speech just for the sake of telling a story; the story must always help you make the point you want to convey to your audience.

(4) Don't make a short story too long.

(5) Be certain that your story will offend absolutely no one in your audience. Make sure your jokes are always in good taste.

It is a good idea to test your jokes or humorous anecdotes out on close friends and family. If you don't get a laugh from them, then your story or joke isn't as funny as you thought it was and you should delete it from your speech. Your close friends and family aren't necessarily your severest critics.

One more caution: Do not employ wit in your speech just for the sake of being funny. Relate an amusing anecdote or tell a joke only to help you make a point. If necessary, explain to your audience the connection between your joke or anecdote and the serious point you are making. Otherwise the audience may remember the joke but forget the point.

13. SUMMING UP

Here, in abbreviated form, are the guides we have discussed in this section.

1. Make your appearance pleasing to your audience.

2. Your posture must at all times inspire respect in your audience.

3. Your voice is an instrument that you can train to deliver your speech effectively and pleasingly.

4. Speak clearly so that your audience hears every word you say. Speak up and out, directly to your audience, never away from it, and relax. Be courteous on stage and maintain eye contact.

5. Rehearse delivering your speech. Memorize it or your outline, plus the opening and closing remarks. If you memorize the whole speech, be careful not to let your delivery become mechanical.

6. Change the tone, tempo, and pitch of your voice to stress a point or to achieve a variety of sound in your speech.

7. Don't be afraid to pause on occasion, for dramatic effect or to let your audience contemplate an important point in your speech.

8. Study your gestures. Be sure they don't drown your talk. Don't let them become wooden or mechanical.

9. Witticisms may aid your speech but be certain they are in good taste and will offend no one.

Section III.
Debating

A debate is a formalized discussion in which speakers take opposing views or sides of an issue or a question. Such a question might be the pros and cons of national health insurance or any other topic of current interest that is controversial.

Debating teams generally consist of two debaters and an alternate debater. The two debaters do the speaking for the team, while the alternates take notes on the discussion and give advice to the speakers.

The topic of the debate is stated in the form of a resolution, also sometimes called a proposition:

"Resolved that our military budget should be cut."

"Resolved that our school increase all extramural athletic competition."

One team of debaters will argue for the resolution. This team will take on the Affirmative side of the debate. The team opposed to the resolution will take on the Negative side. The object of both teams is to "win" the debate by presenting the best arguments for their side. To do this, a team must be prepared to be convincing for its own side, but it must also be prepared to counter the arguments of the opposing side.

This requires a lot of preparation, much digging up of facts, figures, and opinions of people whose opinions are important. Where do you get all this data? Again, the best place to go for this research is your library.

You may find some books in the library dealing with the subject you are to debate. But more likely, you will have to hunt for information in newspaper and magazine articles. The best way to find those articles is to consult an index in the library. *The Readers' Guide to Periodical Literature,* for example, will tell you where to find what you want in magazines. Special newspaper indexes will tell you where to find articles in the pages of various newspapers. And there are other indexes you may be able to use, such as the *Agricultural Index,* the *Engineering Index,* and the *Education Index* plus a tremendous number of other reference books you might find useful. If you have any difficulty getting to the material you need, remember the librarian is there to help you.

Whenever you find material you think you need, do precisely what you did for your written speech. Write down the information, marking exactly where you got it. If you are going to quote a professional opinion, be sure you copy the quotation exactly and the date and place it was said.

Once you have all your information, proceed as you did with your written speech, this time together with your debating partner. Divide your facts, figures, major points, and minor points between you. Then write your speeches out or, since in a debate you are not allowed to read your speeches, write out careful notes.

This is half the job. As was said earlier, the debater must also be well prepared to counter, deny, or disprove the arguments of the opposition. To do this you must acquaint yourself with all the arguments your opposition is likely to make, and have on hand data, figures, and quotations that can refute them.

For this purpose you will again use the library and its indexes and again prepare a thorough set of notes. The better you are prepared with your own arguments and with your refutation, the more likely you are to win the debate.

The actual debate is usually quite formalized. There is a chairperson in charge. The Affirmative team sits on one side of the platform, the Negative on the other side.

The chairperson calls the meeting to order, announces the question (resolution) under debate, then calls on the Affirmative to speak.

The speaking has its order, too. The speakers alternate taking the stand—first the Affirmative, then the Negative. This order is reversed when the teams take the floor for rebuttal (to refute or prove false the arguments of the opposition).

In debating, you follow all the rules for delivering a good speech plus one. That one is that you must listen very carefully to every argument your opponents make and to make a note of those arguments you can refute. Refute those arguments in your rebuttal. Forget the arguments your opposition might have made and didn't.

Following the rebuttal, each side sums up its arguments, the Affirmative first and then the Negative.

There will be a limited time allowed for the summary. Don't repeat your entire speech. Rather, repeat the strongest points your side of the debate made, and mention those arguments that best refute the arguments of your opponents.

Judges are sometimes assigned to declare the winner of the debate. At other times, the audience will vote on the winner. In either case, it will be the side that is better prepared and delivers the best speeches in the most convincing manner that will emerge the victor. It is the logic of a debater's argument and the manner of the delivery that make a winner.

Section IV. Parliamentary Procedure

Almost every meeting is run according to a number of long-established rules and regulations that insure a well-conducted and orderly meeting. These rules and regulations are called parliamentary procedure. A knowledge of parliamentary procedure will help make you a better speaker at club meetings and such.

According to parliamentary procedure, every meeting has an elected chairperson, such as the president of the class or the club, or a temporary chairperson appointed by the president for a specific meeting. On occasion, a chairperson is elected by an informal vote of those present at the meeting.

The responsibility of the chairperson is to direct the meeting and to run it in an orderly fashion. He or she opens the meeting, closes it, and gives the floor to the different people who wish to speak at the meeting. No one may address the meeting until recognized (called on to speak) by the chairperson.

Generally, the chairperson has no vote at the meeting, except when a vote ends in a tie. At such times, he or she may cast the tie-breaking ballot. It is the chairperson who, generally, announces the result of any balloting at the meeting.

Every meeting also has its secretary, elected or appointed. The secretary records and reads the minutes. Minutes are the written record of exactly what happened in a meeting, including the different reports made by members of the meeting, the nature of any discussions at the meeting, and the different decisions taken at the meeting.

In accordance with proper procedure, then, the chairperson opens the meeting:

"I call the meeting of the Junior Stamp Collectors Club to order."

And then, "The secretary will please read the minutes."

The secretary reads the minutes from the previous meeting, then the chairperson asks, "Are there any corrections or additions?" That is, have there been any errors or omissions in the secretary's minutes?

If you, at the meeting, wish to point out an error or omission, you will raise your hand to speak. But you will speak only after you have been recognized by the chairperson.

Following any discussion on the minutes, the chairperson will say, "The minutes are accepted as read," if there are no corrections made, or, if corrections are made, "The minutes are accepted as corrected."

The chairperson then asks, "Is there any old business?"

Old business (also called "matters arising") is "unfinished" business to which the meeting has to attend. It might be a report on, say, the cost of uniforms, or the expenses involved in a picnic. It might be the need to conclude the discussion that had not come to a vote in the previous meeting.

Once this unfinished business is out of the way, the chairperson asks, "Is there any new business?"

New business, obviously, will involve questions and problems that have not been previously discussed by the meeting.

Now suppose you want your class, school, or club to start a clean-up campaign, to raise funds for some local charity, or to create a chess team. You ask the chairperson for the floor. You are recognized. You bring up the idea.

"With all the graffiti in the school halls and on the cafeteria walls, what do you think about a clean-up campaign?"

The question will begin a discussion, an orderly discussion, as the chairperson recognizes one speaker at a time.

Following the discussion, before the meeting can make a decision on the question, there must be a formal statement on the question. The formal statement is called a "motion."

"I move that this club organize a schoolwide clean-up campaign."

The chairperson repeats the motion: "The motion is that this club organize a schoolwide clean-up campaign."

And adds, "Does anyone second the motion?"

To "second a motion" generally means to approve of the motion. A motion needs to be seconded by someone before it can be formally discussed or come to a vote.

Let us say that this motion is seconded. The chairperson then asks, "Is there any discussion?"

The discussion follows, the speakers speaking, pro and con, one at a time, as the chairperson recognizes each speaker.

At one point in the discussion, when all the arguments, pro and con, seem to have been made, someone at the meeting will say, "I call the question."

"I call the question" means "I call for a vote on the motion under discussion."

The chairperson responds.

"The question has been called. Do I have a second?"

The "calling of the question" must, like the motion itself, be seconded.

Following the "second," the chairperson calls for a vote on whether or not to end the discussion of the question.

"Those in favor, say 'Aye'."

Those who approve the motion will respond.

The chairperson then asks for those opposed, and those who want the discussion to continue will vote "No."

If the noes are in the majority, the discussion continues until there are enough ayes to move for a vote. If the ayes are in the majority, the chairperson proceeds to a vote on the question by first repeating the proposal (in this case, the organizing of a clean-up campaign), then asking again for a vote: those for the motion, those against.

Whichever way the ballot is taken, by voice vote, by a show of hands, or by secret ballot, the chairperson makes the announcement of the result of the voting:

"The motion is carried" or "The motion is defeated."

In some cases, before a vote can be taken, someone at the meeting may offer an amendment, a change in the original motion.

For example, if the original motion calls for a schoolwide clean-up campaign, a speaker might ask that the motion be amended to read "clubmember clean-up campaign." The amendment must be seconded.

If the person who made the original motion is willing to accept the change suggested, then the motion itself is changed. If he or she does not accept the amendment, then the amendment must be voted on before there is balloting on the original motion.

In other words, the meeting will first vote on whether it wants a clubmember clean-up campaign. If the vote is aye, then the original motion is dead. If it is no, then the vote on the original motion takes place.

There are times, in such procedures, when a meeting cannot come to a decision. It may need more facts or figures. It may need to know the projected expenditures of a campaign or whether permission for such a campaign will be granted. It may question the chances of success for a campaign. At such times, there may be a request to "table the discussion."

To "table a discussion" does not mean to kill the motion. It simply asks for time to collect whatever is necessary for a more intelligent vote, to be held at the next meeting, or at the one following that.

"Tabling a motion," like all other motions, requires the formal request: "I move we table the motion," a seconding of the motion, and an affirmative vote from the meeting.

Another item in parliamentary procedure: If at any time you think the chairperson has allowed a violation of procedure, you may make that known by calling out, "Point of order." Actually, what you are saying is that the chairperson is not conducting the meeting in an "orderly"—according to proper procedure—fashion.

When the chairperson gives you the floor on a point of order, you might say:

"The speaker is not talking on the motion we are discussing."

Or, "You are permitting a speaker to speak on a motion that has not been seconded."

If the chairperson agrees with your "point," he or she will correct the error; if not, he or she will say as much.

If you disagree with the chairperson's judgment, you may appeal that judgment by asking for a vote by the entire meeting on your point of order. Both you and the chairperson, in such cases, must accept the decision made by the entire meeting.

One last item: The chairperson does not end the meeting whenever he or she feels like doing it. A motion to adjourn is required, the motion coming from someone else at the meeting. Again, this motion must be seconded before a vote on closing the meeting can be taken.

Generally, there is no discussion on this motion. The chairperson simply asks for a vote and, with the majority agreeing to an adjournment, announces, "The meeting is adjourned."

There are some times when the members of the meeting want the meeting to continue. They may want an immediate decision made on a particular question. In such cases, they may be able to vote down the motion to adjourn and keep the meeting going until they are ready to close it, all in an orderly and proper manner.

Actually, the rules and regulations for conducting a meeting are simple. Following them becomes mechanical after a while. But knowing and adhering to them will surely make you a more effective speaker, at whatever meeting or assembly you speak.

Index

About the Author

Henry Gilfond is the author of many fine books for young readers, including the popular *Genealogy: How to Find Your Roots* (an Impact Book) for Franklin Watts.

Mr. Gilfond, a former junior high school teacher and editor of literary and dance journals, has also done writing for radio and television. He lives in Shinnecock Hills and New York with his wife Edythe, a costume designer.